FAITH on Trial

STUDIES
FROM THE
LETTER
OF JAMES

ECS
MINISTRIES
The Word to the World

Published By:
ECS Ministries
P.O. Box 1028
Dubuque, IA 52004-1028
www.ecsministries.org

First Edition: 2005
ISBN 1-59387-044-2

Copyright © 2005 ECS Ministries

All rights reserved. No part of this publication may be reproduced or transmitted in any form or by any means, electronic or mechanical, including photocopying and recording, or by any information storage and retrieval system, including the Internet, without the prior written permission of the publisher, with the exception of brief quotations embodied in critical articles or reviews.

All Scripture quotations, unless otherwise indicated, are taken from the New King James Version. Copyright © 1979, 1980, 1982 by Thomas Nelson, Inc. Used by permission. All rights reserved

Printed in the United States of America

Contents

How to Use This Guide — 5

1. Meeting James and His 1st Century Readers — 7
James 1:1

2. Growing Through Trials — 13
James 1:2–12

3. Resisting Temptation — 19
James 1:13–27

4. Purging Partiality — 27
James 2:1–13

5. Living Out Living Faith — 33
James 2:14–26

6. Training the Tongue — 39
James 3:1–12

7. Wising Up to Wisdom — 45
James 3:13–18

8. Curing Conflicts — 51
James 4:1–10

9. Eliminating Arrogance — 59
James 4:11–17

10. Enduring Oppression — 63
James 5:1–12

11. Praying, Confessing, and Caring — 71
James 5:13–20

12. Reviewing James Together — 77

How To Use This Study Guide

The Study Questions

Every member of the study group should have their own copy of this study guide to use in preparing ahead of time for each group study.

The study questions include observation (what does it say?), interpretation (what does it mean?), and application (how does it work in my life?) questions. The questions are based on the Bible text and, for the most part, parallel the material in "The Letter of James" Emmaus study course. You will notice that each study includes a brief introduction with blocks of text interspersed among the questions. These are direct quotations from the Emmaus course. Some have been included to instruct, some to enlighten, some to challenge, and some to simply enrich. Reading the complete course material will help your own preparation, but it is not required for answering the questions. Most of the personal "Take the Test" questions are also taken from the Emmaus study course. These questions are intended for personal reflection and application.

The Group Study

Begin each study asking God the Holy Spirit to guide and to teach. The leader should moderate the discussion, redirecting questions rather than answering them. The study course may be referred to if further explanation is needed.

We recommend that each person takes a question in turn, sharing their prepared answer. This method eliminates the silences that usually follow questions that are posed to a group as a whole. Also, all the group members are more likely to come prepared. The leader can open up each question for discussion to everyone once it has been initially answered. All Scriptures given with the questions should be read and used as the basis for answering the questions in the study guide.

STUDY ONE

James 1: 1

MEETING JAMES AND HIS 1ST CENTURY READERS

Faith on Trial

Most evangelical Christians assume it was James, the Lord's brother [who wrote this letter], but we cannot be certain. We can be glad that this in no way affects the inspiration of the letter, or the benefit we can get from it.... If the author of this letter was the Lord's brother ... then a wonderful change had come in his life. At one time, he had not believed in the Lord Jesus. He may have shared the prevalent view that Jesus was out of His mind. But our Lord patiently sowed the seed of the Word. Though unappreciated, He taught the great principles of the Kingdom of God. Then the seed took root in the life of James. A mighty transformation resulted. The skeptic became a servant. And he wasn't ashamed to say so!

Read the entire Letter of James in one sitting.

1. What do we learn about James, the Lord's brother, from the following Scriptures? Matthew 13:55; Mark 3:21; John 7:3-5; Acts 15:13 (in the context of the whole chapter); 1 Corinthians 15:5, 7.

2. How does James describe himself (v. 1)? What does this description indicate about his character?

3. Have you made any other observations about the man James from his letter? If so, what lesson(s) can you draw from those observations?

The letter is addressed to the "twelve tribes [of Israel] which are scattered abroad," or "which are of the Dispersion." These people were Jews by birth.... In Acts 8:1, we read that the early Christians ... were scattered abroad throughout Judea and Samaria by the persecutions of Saul. This dispersion is referred to again where we read that believers were driven to Phenice (Phoenicia), Cyprus and Antioch.

3a. When we take into account the historical situation referred to above and the ongoing oppression by the Roman government, what can we infer about the material, emotional, and social circumstances of the Christian Jews to whom James wrote (v. 1)?

3b. What evidence is there within the letter itself that these people were suffering hardships as a result of their conversion to Christianity?

3c. Although our circumstances may be very different today, in what sense(s) can we identify with these early believers? See Philippians 3:20 and Hebrews 11:13-16.

Faith on Trial

> *"Faith on trial" is the theme of this letter. Within its five short chapters, James puts our faith to the test. He wants to know if it is genuine or a cheap imitation.... This letter is strangely silent concerning the great fundamental doctrines of the Christian faith [like the incarnation].... But this is not strange at all. The writer's purpose was not to teach doctrine so much as to show us how the Word should become incarnate in our lives.... This he has done exceedingly well.*

4a. What topics and themes stand out to you?

4b. Which specific words and terms appear frequently?

> *There are frequent references to the law in this letter.... James does not teach that his readers are under law for salvation or as a rule of life. Rather, portions of the law are cited as instruction in righteousness for those who are under grace.*

Meeting James and His 1st Century Readers

5. The letter's 108 verses contain about fifty imperatives (commands). What does this imply about at least one reason James had for writing it?

6. What different styles and tones does James use to motivate these believers to live out their professed faith in Christ? (For example, asking rhetorical questions in 2:14-26 to challenge; giving encouragement in 1:12)

7. Comment on the relevance of the Letter of James to believers today. What is your initial overall response?

8. Write here any questions about the letter you have at this point that you hope to have answered by the conclusion of the study.

STUDY TWO

James 1: 2–12

GROWING THROUGH TRIALS

Faith on Trial

In [the first] section [of this chapter] James deals with the subject of temptation. He uses the word in two different senses. In verses 2-12, the temptations are what we might call holy trials or problems which are sent from God and which test the reality of our faith and produce likeness to Christ. In verses 13-17, on the other hand, the subject is unholy temptations, which come from within and which lead to sin.

1a. Define the word *trial*. Give at least five different examples, categories, or levels of trials.

1b. Do you believe that all trials "test the reality of our faith" (see introduction above)? Are any trials or problems outside the bounds of being relevant to growing spiritually? Support your answer.

2. What different attitudes might James's readers have towards their difficult circumstances, and which one are they (and we) exhorted to have? (v. 2; see Hebrews 12:5).

A better word for patience here would be steadfastness or fortitude. As our faith is put to the test, we become strengthened to meet problems still to come. We may liken the process to a tree that is exposed to the winter gales. The pressure of the gales causes the roots to go down deeper and the tree itself becomes stronger. Without problems we would never develop endurance.

3. What is God's purpose in allowing His people to go through trials? (vv. 3-4; see Hebrews 12:11).

4a. Which aspects of God's character are we putting our faith in when we ask for wisdom (vv. 5-8)? What connection do you see between what we learn about God in verse 17 and these verses?

4b. What part does knowledge play in using wisdom?

4c. Using the definition of wisdom given below, give a true-to-life example of how verse 5 works in practice.

Faith on Trial

The Bible does not give specific answers to the innumerable problems that arise in life. It does not solve problems in so many words, but God's Word does give us general principles. We must apply these principles to problems as they arise day by day. That is why we need wisdom. 'Spiritual wisdom is the practical application in the daily life of the teaching of Jesus Christ.'

5a. What does "double-minded" mean (vv. 6-8)?

5b. Why do you think this is treated as such a serious fault in a believer? Why will this person not receive wisdom from God?

5c. What is the warning to us?

Whether a man is poor or rich, he can derive lasting spiritual benefits from the calamities and crises of life.

---

6. What are the attitude(s) a poor believer is exhorted to have to his circumstances (v. 9)? How is this man a good illustration of verses 3-5?

Growing Through Trials

7. Describe the mature, spiritual attitude of a believer who has lost his wealth (vv. 10-11) that would demonstrate his genuine faith in Christ.

8a. How is "the man" of verse 12 described?

8b. In what way is this verse an encouragement to the reader?

Everyone's cup will be full in heaven, but people will have different sized cups, that is, different capacities for enjoying heaven. This is doubtless what is in view in the expression "crown of life"; it refers to a fuller enjoyment of the glories of heaven.

---

9. Share with the group a trial where you applied the principles in verses 2–12 and through which you matured in your faith. As a group, spend a few minutes in prayer giving glory to God for His wisdom and goodness.

10. Are you going through a trial right now? What teachings in the Bible relate to it? Have you asked God for the wisdom and grace you need to mature spiritually through the experience?

FAITH ON TRIAL

Putting My Faith to the Test

How do we react when various forms of testing come into our lives?

- Do we complain bitterly against the misfortunes of life, or do we rejoice and thank the Lord for them?

- Do we advertise our trials or do we bear them quietly?

- Do we live in the future, waiting for our circumstances to improve, or do we live in the present, seeking to see the hand of God in all that comes to us?

- Do we indulge in self-pity and seek sympathy or do we submerge self in a life of service for others?

STUDY THREE

James 1: 13–27

RESISTING
TEMPTATION

> *The subject now shifts to unholy temptations.... Man is always ready to shift responsibility for his sins. If he cannot blame God he will adopt the approach of modern psychology by saying that sin is a sickness. In this way he hopes to escape judgment. But sin is not a sickness; it is a moral failure.*

1a. How does temptation to sin differ from testing in both its origin and its intent (v. 13)?

1b. Why is it important that we remember that God does not tempt us to sin? What light does verse 17 shed?

2. To what natural process does James liken being tempted to sin (v. 15)? Explain the process.

> *The word for lusts [NKJV "desires"] in verse 14 could refer to any form of desire, good or evil. The word itself is morally neutral. But with few exceptions it is used in the New Testament to describe evil desires, and that is certainly the case here.*

Resisting Temptation

3. What kinds of "evil desires" are the suffering Christian more likely to be tempted by?

4. (Optional) Give an example from personal experience of a victory over a temptation to sin that was connected to a trial you were going through. Explain the part that God's Word, a fellow Christian, the indwelling Spirit of God, or circumstances played in the experience.

> *Sin ... leads to eternal, spiritual death—the final separation of the person from God and from spiritual blessing.... There is a sense also in which sin results in death for a believer. For instance, in 1 Timothy 5:6 we read that a believing widow who lives in pleasure is dead while she lives. This means that she is wasting her life and utterly failing to fulfill the purpose for which God saved her. To be out of fellowship with God is for a Christian a form of living death.*

5a. In contrast to the death that sin generates, verse 18 describes another kind of "process," in which God generates productive life. Using actual phrases in verse 18, answer the following questions as they apply to James's original readers.

❖ *What did God do and what prompted Him?*

❖ *How and to what end?*

5b. How does verse 18 apply to us today?

6a. In verses 19-22 James gives some examples of actions and attitudes that will give evidence of having been born from above. What are they?

6b. How is the principle in verse 20 relevant to what James has been saying to his original readers about their trials and temptations?

The Bible is the instrument God uses in the new birth. He uses it in saving the soul not only from the penalty of sin, but from its power as well. He uses it in saving us not only from damnation in eternity, but from damage in this life. It is doubtless this present, continuing aspect of salvation which James is speaking of in verse 21.

---

7. Describe how the illustration of the mirror (vv. 23-25) pictures (a) how we should respond to God's Word and (b) how we should not respond to God's Word.

Resisting Temptation

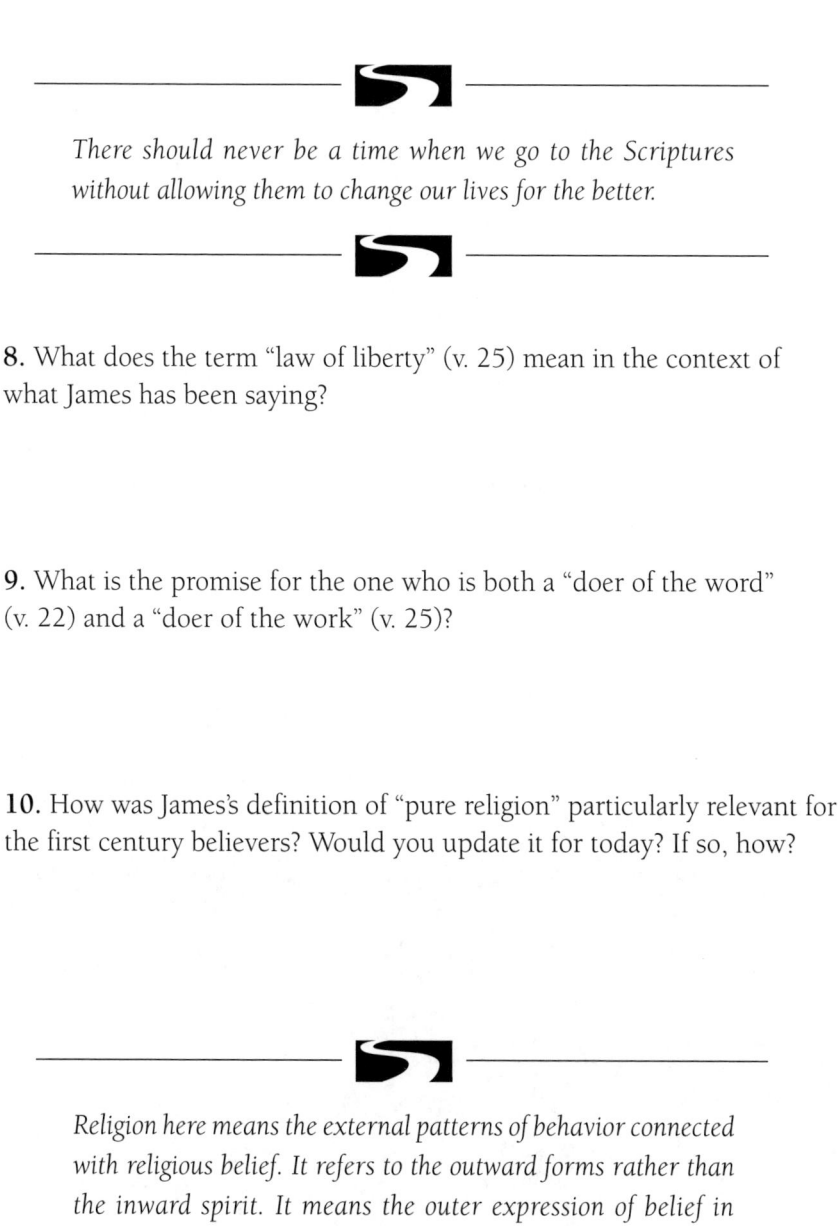

> *There should never be a time when we go to the Scriptures without allowing them to change our lives for the better.*

8. What does the term "law of liberty" (v. 25) mean in the context of what James has been saying?

9. What is the promise for the one who is both a "doer of the word" (v. 22) and a "doer of the work" (v. 25)?

10. How was James's definition of "pure religion" particularly relevant for the first century believers? Would you update it for today? If so, how?

> *Religion here means the external patterns of behavior connected with religious belief. It refers to the outward forms rather than the inward spirit. It means the outer expression of belief in worship and service rather than to the doctrines believed.*

11. James warns us three times in this passage not to deceive ourselves (vv. 16, 22, 26). By way of review, what are the things he is referring to?

12. Look back over chapter 1. List the different ways (negative and positive) in which we can respond to God and His Word. How do you rate your own personal response to Him in light of these observations?

Resisting Temptation

Putting My Faith to the Test

- Do we encourage evil thoughts to linger in our minds, or do we expel them quickly?

- When we sin, do we say that we couldn't help it?

- Do we blame God when we are tempted to sin?

- Do I read the Bible with a humble desire to have God rebuke me, teach me and change me?

- Am I anxious to have my tongue bridled?

- Do I justify my temper or do I want victory over it?

- How do I react when someone starts to tell an off-color joke?

- Does my faith manifest itself in deeds of kindness to those who cannot repay me?

STUDY FOUR

James 2:1–13

PURGING
PARTIALITY

Faith on Trial

Favoritism is utterly foreign to the example of the Lord or to the teachings of the New Testament. There is no place in Christianity for snobbishness or discrimination.

1. From the following verses (and any others that you know), state why it wrong for Christians to show partiality. James 1:27 -2:1; Deuteronomy 10:17-19; Romans 3:22-23; Galatians 3:28.

2. What kinds of discrimination exist in our society? In our community? Among Christians?

3. Who is being favored and who is being discriminated against in the illustration James uses in verses 2-3?

4. Why do you think James calls the Lord Jesus Christ "glorious" (v.1) in this context?

5. What have we become when we show partiality (v. 4)?

PURGING PARTIALITY

> *Repeatedly we find in Scripture that it is the poor people, not the rich, who rally to the banner of Christ...Rich people are ordinarily poor in faith because they trust their riches instead of the Lord. On the other hand, poor people have been chosen by God to be rich in faith.*

6a. List the four reasons James gave these 1st century believers why they should not favor the rich and dishonor the poor.

    vv. 5-6a

    v. 6b

    v. 7

    vv. 8-9

6b. Are these reasons still valid today? Support your answer.

> *The law of love is called the royal law because it belongs to the King and because it is the king of laws. To show respect of persons is a violation of the royal law.... Certain acts are sinful because they are basically and inherently wrong, but they become transgressions when there is a specific law which forbids them. Partiality is sinful because it is essentially wrong in itself. But it is also transgression because there is a law against it.*

7. What is the principle in verses 10-11? What point is James making as it relates to partiality (v. 9)?

> *The teachings of the Lord Jesus ... actually call for a higher standard of conduct than the law required.... [James] is not saying, "If you show respect of persons, you are breaking the law, and are thus condemned to death." What he is saying is, "As believers, you are no longer under the law of bondage, but you are under the law of liberty—liberty to do what is right."*

8a. Read verses 8 and 12 along with James 1:22 and 25. What do these verses teach are the solutions to the issue?

8b. Submitting ourselves to the law of liberty again, how do the following verses apply to our obeying the command about discrimination? See Matthew 7:1-2; Matthew 25:40; 2 Corinthians 5:10; Hebrews 13:2.

[Verse 13] may mean we can rejoice in the face of judgment if we have shown mercy to others.... Or it may mean that mercy triumphs over judgment in the sense that it is always greater than judgment. The general idea seems to be that if we show mercy to others, the judgment which might otherwise fall on us will be replaced by mercy.

---

9. Is the Lord speaking to you on this subject? What steps do you need to take, in attitude or action, to obey the Lord in this?

Faith on Trial

Putting My Faith to the Test

- Do we show more kindness to those of our own race than those of other races?

- Are we more kindly disposed to the young than to the old?

- Are we more outgoing to good-looking people than to those who are plain or who dress differently to us?

- Are we more anxious to befriend prominent people than those who are comparatively unknown?

- Do we avoid people with physical infirmities and seek the companionship of the strong and healthy?

- Do we favor the rich over the poor?

- Do we give the "cold shoulder" to "foreigners," to those who speak our language with a foreign accent?

STUDY FIVE

James 2:14–26

LIVING OUT LIVING FAITH

Faith on Trial

> *These verses are perhaps the most controversial in the epistle by James,... [They are] commonly used to support the heresy that we are saved by faith plus works. In other words, we must trust the Lord Jesus as our Savior, but that is not enough. We must also add to His redemptive work our own deeds of charity and devotion.*

1. How many question marks do you count in this passage? How many rhetorical questions? What does that indicate about James's approach and what he is trying to do here?

2. The full principle on which James's argument is based is covered in verses 17 and 24. Summarize that principle here in your own words.

3. To be justified before God means to have a right standing before Him, to be counted righteous and acceptable to God in a legal sense. What do we learn from the following verses about the doctrine of justification?

    Romans 3:24

    Romans 5:1

    Romans 8:33

    James 2:24

Curing Conflicts

4. How would you describe the faith of the person in verse 14?

5a. How does James illustrate the futility of words without actions (vv. 15-16)?

5b. Considering the kinds of trials his original readers were going through, comment on James' choice of illustration.

5c. "Works," "deeds," and "actions" are not confined to showing charity to the needy. Using James' main principle, create an appropriate illustration that would be very relevant to today's community of believers.

> James is not saying that we are saved by faith plus works. To hold such a view would be to dishonor the finished work of the Lord Jesus Christ. If we were saved by faith and by works, then there would be two saviors—Jesus and ourselves. But the New Testament is very clear that Christ is the one and only Savior.... Works are not the root of salvation but the fruit; they are not the cause but the effect.

---

6. How do we prove that our faith in God is genuine saving faith (v. 18)?

7a. How does verse 19 lend further support to the point James is making?

7b. What is the difference between demons belief about God, and saving faith?

8a. How was Abraham justified before God? (v. 23; see Genesis 15:6)

8b. How did Abraham prove that his faith was genuine? (v. 21; see Genesis 22).

8c. What makes Abraham an excellent example of what James is teaching in this passage (v. 22)?

9. Describe the relationship between Rahab's faith and her actions (v. 25; see Joshua 2).

Living Out Living Faith

Some people use this passage to prove that salvation is by good works. But what they mean by good works is giving to charity, paying your debts, telling the truth and going to church. Were these the good works of Abraham and Rahab? They certainly were not. In Abraham's case, it was willingness to kill his son! In Rahab's case, it was treason! If you remove the element of faith from these works, they would be evil rather than good.... Mackintosh well says, "This section refers to life-works, not law-works.... Look at them as the fruit of faith and they were life-works."

10. What characteristics are common to all three of James's illustrations in terms of defining an action that makes faith "perfect" or "complete"?

11a. What comparison does James make in verse 26 to summarize what he has been saying about faith and actions?

11b. What is the logical conclusion from this passage about someone who claims to have faith but does not demonstrate it in any form?

11c. What is the challenge for true believers? Are you a genuine believer?

Faith on Trial

Putting My Faith to the Test

- ✒ Do I keep a modest wardrobe in order to share clothing with those who do not have enough?

- ✒ Do I live sacrificially in order to be able to send the gospel to those who are starving for the Bread of Life?

- ✒ Do I go out of my way to serve others, or do I just do what fits into my schedule?

- ✒ Am I willing, like Abraham, to offer the dearest thing in my life to God?

- ✒ Am I willing, like Rahab, to turn traitor to the world in order to be loyal to Christ?

STUDY SIX

James 3:1–12

TRAINING THE TONGUE

Faith on Trial

Just as an old fashioned doctor examined a patient's tongue to assist in diagnosis, so James tests a person's spiritual health by his conversation.... James would agree with the modern wit who said, "Watch your tongue. It is in a wet place where it is easy to slip."

---

1. This passage on the tongue is not the first time James has addressed the topic. What righteous or unrighteous use of the tongue have we seen so far?

    1:5

    1:6

    1:13

    1:19

    1:26

    2:3

    2:7

Training the Tongue

   2:14; 2:18

   2:16

2. Of the works of the flesh listed in Galatians 5:19-21, which are related to the use of the tongue?

3. Why is control of the tongue such an important issue for the believer? See Matthew 12:36-37 and Colossians 3:17.

The phrase "Let not many of you become teachers" may be paraphrased "Do not become unduly ambitious to be a teacher." This should not be interpreted as a prohibition against the use of his gift by one who has actually been called of God to teach.

---

4. Why should the responsibility of teaching God's Word not be undertaken lightly? (vv. 1-2)

5. Describe the positive and the negative effects that a teacher's influence can have.

Faith on Trial

6. In James 3:3-8 we are given five similes (illustrations) of the tongue and its power. What does each one teach us?

    1. **Bridle** (v. 3)

    2. **Rudder** (v. 4)

    3. **Fire** (vv. 5-6)

    4. **Wild animals** (v. 7)

    5. **Poison** (v. 8)

Who can measure the harm that has been done, the tears that have flowed, the hearts that have been broken, the reputations that have been ruined. And who can measure the misery it has brought to our own lives and to our families; the inward bitterness that has been aroused; the shame of having to apologize; the bad effects on our physical health. Parents who have openly indulged in criticism of fellow-believers have had to watch their children adopt the same critical spirit and wander off from Christian fellowship. The price we have to pay for undisciplined use of our tongue is enormous.

Training the Tongue

7. What point is James making in verse 10?

8. What is the principle about speech that James is teaching in the comparisons he gives in verses 11-12? How do they help reinforce his point?

This passage [vv. 9-12] should not be confused with a similar one in Matthew 7:16-20. There we are warned against expecting good fruit from bad trees. Evil men can only produce wicked words. Here we are warned against using the tongue to produce two opposite kinds of fruit.

---

9. List at least three practical things we can do to discipline our tongues to use them for good and not evil.

10. The book of Proverbs has a lot to say about the tongue. Scan Proverbs for verses that give practical instruction on the topic. Try to find three to five verses and write them out here.

Faith on Trial

11. Memorize any of the verses in study six that speak to a weakness in your life.

All that we say should be subject to the threefold test: Is it true? Is it kind? Is it necessary?

Putting My Faith to the Test

- Do I teach others things that I have not obeyed myself?

- Do I criticize others behind their back?

- Is my speech consistently clean, edifying, kind?

- Do I use language like gosh, golly, jeez, heck, good heavens?

- After a solemn meeting do I joke with friends? Talk about football scores?

- In retelling a story, do I exaggerate in order to make people more impressed?

STUDY SEVEN

James 3:13–18

WISING UP TO WISDOM

Faith on Trial

> *When James speaks about wisdom, he is not thinking of how much knowledge a man has in his head, but how he lives his life from day to day. It is not the possession of knowledge but the proper application of it that counts.... The truly wise man is the one who manifests the life of Christ, the man in whom the fruit of the Spirit is evident.... The worldly-wise man ... acts according to the principles of this world. He embodies all the traits that men glorify. His behavior gives no evidence of divine life within.*

1. What value did the Old Testament (on which these Jewish believers would have been raised) put on divine wisdom (Proverbs 4:7)?

2. What is the relationship between wisdom and understanding, and humility (v. 13)? Scan the first few chapters of Proverbs for extra insights.

3. Why is this passage in James particularly relevant to teachers of God's Word (v. 14; compare v. 1)?

4a. Draw a comparison between the two kinds of wisdom James describes in verses 14-18.

Wising Up To Wisdom

	DIVINE WISDOM	**WORLDLY WISDOM**
Where it comes from		
How it's characterized		
What it produces		

4b. Discuss in the group any of these terms you do not understand.

5. In what sense is it possible to lie against (deny) the truth when we are teaching or professing it verbally (v. 14)?

> We must constantly guard against allowing worldly principles to guide us in spiritual affairs. James calls this false wisdom earthly, sensual and devilish (v. 15). There is an intended downward climax in these three adjectives. Earthly means that this wisdom is not from heaven; it is from this earth. Sensual means that it is not the fruit of the Holy Spirit, but of man's lower nature. Devilish means that it stoops to actions that resemble the behavior of demons rather than men.

---

6. How might the three terms describing this world's wisdom be evident in our Christian circles?

7. In a positional sense, true believers are not "of this world" (John 17:16), so what is the practical warning of this passage (a) for believers generally and (b) especially for those who teach or want to teach God's Word (v. 1)?

A wise man will love peace, and he will do all he can to maintain peace without sacrificing purity. This is illustrated by Luther's story of two goats that met on a narrow bridge over deep water. They would not go back and they did not dare to fight. "After a short parley, one of them lay down and let the other go over him, and thus no harm was done, The moral," Luther would say, "is easy: be content if thy person is trod upon for peace's sake; thy person, I say, not thy conscience."

---

8. Read Genesis 12:10-20, an incident in Abraham's life where he used worldly wisdom. How does this passage in James parallel that situation?

9. At the group meeting, divide into twos and spend a few minutes coming up with a scenario where any or all of the godly characteristics of divine wisdom would shine. Share these scenarios with one another.

Verse 18 is a connecting link between what we have been discussing and what is to follow. We have just learned that true wisdom is peace-loving. In the next chapter we find conflict among God's people. Here we are reminded that life is like the farming process. We have the farmer (the wise man who is a peace maker), the climate (peace) and the harvest (righteousness). The farmer wants to raise a harvest of righteousness. Can this be done in an atmosphere of quarrels and bickering? No, the sowing must take place under peaceful conditions. A harvest of uprightness will be produced in their own lives and in the lives of those to whom they minister.

Putting My Faith to the Test

- Do I respect the proud men of the world more than the humble believer in the Lord Jesus?

- Do I serve the Lord without caring who gets the credit?

- Do I sometimes use questionable means in order to get good results?

- Am I guilty of flattery in order to influence people?

- Do I harbor jealousy and resentment in my heart?

- Do I resort to sarcasm and unkind remarks?

- Am I pure in thought, in speech, in morals?

STUDY EIGHT

James 4: 1–10

CURING
CONFLICTS

Faith on Trial

Why are there so many unhappy homes and so many assemblies torn by division? Why are there such bitter feuds among Christian workers in the homeland, and such conflicts among missionaries abroad? The reason is that we are ceaselessly striving to satisfy our lust for pleasures and possessions, and to outdo others.

---

1. Describe James's tone in this section. What do you think is his goal in using this approach?

2. List the sins, both specified and implied, in verses 1-10. State whether they are inward or outward sins and what their relationship is to one another, if any.

3. What is the source of all conflicts? (vv. 1-2a; cf. Romans 7:22-23, Galatians 5:19-21; 1 Peter 2:11).

4. What are some ways we tend to justify or rationalize what we want to happen in our local congregations?

5. What light does Jesus' teaching in Matthew 5:21-22 shed on the use of the word "murder" in verse 2? What do you think is the general thrust of this verse?

6. Why are these desires so futile—as well as dangerous—to a congregation's spiritual condition? See James 1:19-20 and Galatians 5:15.

7a. In dealing with these desires, (a) what are James's readers not doing, and (b) what are they doing wrong? (vv. 2-3).

7b. Read again James 1; 5, 13, and 17. How do those verses relate to this section?

The world is the system which man has built up for himself in an effort to satisfy the lust of the eyes, the lust of the flesh, and the pride of life [1 John 2:15-17]. In this system there is no room for God or for His Son. It maybe the world of art, of culture, of education, of science, or even of religion.... How unthinkable it is that believers should ever want to walk arm-in-arm with the world that murdered their Savior!

8a. What point is James driving home in verse 4? What is the connection between this verse and verses 1-3?

8b. What is our clear choice and challenge?

Verse 5 is one of the most difficult in the epistle.... While the exact words are not found in the Old Testament, James may have been quoting them as being the general teaching of the Scripture.... The problem is ... whether the spirit is the Holy Spirit or the spirit of passionate jealousy. If the former is meant, then the thought is that the Holy Spirit which God made to dwell in us does not originate the lust and jealousy which causes strife; rather He yearns over us with jealousy for our entire devotion to Christ. If the latter is intended, then the meaning is that the spirit that dwells in us, (that is, the spirit of lust and envy) is the cause of all our unfaithfulness to God.

---

9. Read verse 6. What is the basis here for James' directives in verses 7 to 10? What does verse 6 teach us about God?

Curing Conflicts

10. If possible, summarize in one word the remedy for the sins that have been condemned in this passage (vv. 7-10)?

11a. In what way do the steps commanded in verse 7b and verse 8 complement each other?

11b. Practically-speaking, what does it mean, to "resist the devil," especially in the context of this chapter?

11c. What is the promise of God's drawing near an evidence of? (See verse 6.)

The hands speak of our actions and the heart represents our motives and desires.

---

12. How does obedience to the command in verse 8 work in practice with respect to the inward sins of anger, envy, and selfish ambition and the outward sins of fights and quarrels (v. 2)?

Faith on Trial

> *This [verses 7-10] is the way we should respond when the Lord exposes us to ourselves. Too often it is not the case, however. Sometimes, for example, we are in a meeting when God speaks loudly to our hearts. We are stirred for the moment, and filled with good resolves. But when the meeting closes, the people engage in animated and light-hearted conversation. The whole atmosphere of the meeting is dispersed, the power is dissipated, and the Spirit of God is quenched.*

13. What point is James making in verse 9?

14. How is verse 10 another evidence of God's grace?

15. Have you experienced or witnessed the above scenario? What steps do you think we can take, whether individually or as a congregation, to facilitate the convicting work of the Spirit of God for ourselves and for others?

Putting My Faith to the Test

✎ Am I continually anxious to have my own way?

✎ Am I willing to come close enough to the Lord to let Him reveal to me the motives of my heart?

✎ When God speaks to me, do I submit or resist?

✎ Do my heart and my actions reveal me to be a friend of God or the world?

STUDY NINE

James 4: 11–17

ELIMINATING ARROGANCE

Faith on Trial

> *Only God is superior to the law; He is the One who gave it and the One who judges by it. Who then has the audacity to usurp the place of God by speaking maliciously against a brother?*

1. What is the sin that James addresses in verses 11 and 12? Do you think there is any connection to the first part of chapter 4? If so, what is it?

2. What logical argument does James give these Jewish believers for not slandering and judging a brother (vv. 11-12)?

3a. What contrast do you see between the attitude and disposition of the person in verse 11 and verse 10?

3b. What is the clear lesson for us?

> *Someone has suggested that there are three questions we should answer before indulging in criticism of others—What good does it do your brother? What good does it do yourself? What glory for God is in it?*

Eliminating Arrogance

4. In what practical ways can you make the wise advice just given a mindset and a regular practice?

5. What are the two reasons it is wrong to make plans for the future independent of God…

> **(a) in relation to yourself** (v. 13, 16; compare v. 6)

> **(b) in relation to your circumstances** (v. 14; see Proverbs 27:1)

6. In what way do the principles about testing and temptation from chapter 1 relate to this section?

7. What should be our attitude to making plans for the future (v. 15)? Read the example the apostle Paul set in 1 Corinthians 4:19.

8. What are some ways we can put this attitude into practice, to do more than say "God willing"?

Faith on Trial

> *To do good [verse 17], in this context, is to take God into every aspect of our lives, to live in moment by moment dependence on Him. If we know we should do this, yet fail to do it, we are clearly sinning.... If we know what is right, we are under obligation to live up to that light.*

9a. What is the meaning of verse 17 as a general principle for the Christian life?

9b. Where can you apply it in relation to what you have been studying (and now know) from James?

Putting My Faith to the Test

✎ Do I speak against my brothers?

✎ Do I make plans without consulting the Lord?

✎ Am I getting caught up in the attraction of materialism?

✎ Am I trusting in the Lord or trusting in my own resources for my future?

STUDY TEN

James 5:1–12

ENDURING OPPRESSION

Faith on Trial

In one of the most searching and piercing sections of his letter, James ... launches into a denunciation of the sins of the rich. The words fall like hammer-blows, blunt and unsparing.... James is here seen in the role of a prophet of social justice. He cries out against the failure of the rich to use their money for the alleviation of human need. He condemns those who have become rich by exploiting their workers. He rebukes their use of wealth for self-indulgence and luxurious living. Finally, he pictures the rich as arrogant oppressors of the righteous.

1. Do you think James is condemning believers or unbelievers when he addresses "you rich" here in chapter 5? What would be the arguments for both interpretations and James's purpose in each case?

2. What four kinds of wealth are mentioned (vv. 2-3)?

3. If being rich is not in itself sinful, what is James condemning in verse 2 and 3? See Matthew 6:19-21.

4. What is the sin described in verse 4?

> [The workers] had no one on earth to plead their cause successfully. However, their cries were heard by the Lord of Sabaoth, that is, the Lord of hosts. He who commands the armies of heaven is strong in behalf of earth's downtrodden masses. The Lord God Omnipotent will help and avenge them.

5. Why is self-indulgence condemned (v. 5)?

> It is probably best to think of "the righteous one" [v. 6] as representing innocent men in general. James is thinking of the rough, high-handed way in which rich people have characteristically behaved toward their subordinates. They have condemned them by false accusation and threats. They have killed them, not directly perhaps, but by overworking and underpaying them. The innocent offered no resistance. To protest might result in further brutality, or dismissal from his job.

6. How is this passage (a) a comfort and (b) a warning to the reader who is suffering at the hands of the ungodly rich?

Faith on Trial

7. Why does James exhort suffering believers to be patient (v. 8; compare v. 4)? Refer back to lesson 2 for the meaning of patience.

8. How does James illustrate the need of patience (v. 7)?

9. What are we exhorted to be patient about in connection with ourselves (v. 7)? See Philippians 1:6; 1 Peter 1:6-7.

10. According to Romans 5:3-5, where does patience fit in the process of growth?

11a. What are we to wait patiently for (vv. 7-8)?

11b. What difference should the Lord's imminent return make to us?

12. What do you think James means by "strengthen our hearts," especially in connection with the return of the Lord (v. 8)?

13. How does the command in verse 9 compare with earlier instructions to do with relationships with fellow-believers?

14. What motivation does James give this time? See 2 Corinthians 5:9-10.

> *During times of persecution and distress, it is not uncommon for the victims to turn against one another. It is a curious twist of human nature that in time of pressure we build up wrath against those we love most.... The word grudge here does not mean to allow reluctantly but rather to have inward resentments that are unexpressed. This verse has a voice for servants of the Lord working together under trying circumstances.*

15a. How are the Old Testament prophets examples of endurance (vv. 10-11)?

15b. In what way are those who have endured (and, by implication, those who endure trials now), "blessed"? What aspects of God's character are of comfort especially (v. 11)?

15c. In contrast, what damage is done in our lives and the lives of those around us if we do not endure times of difficulty patiently?

16. What makes Job a good example of endurance (v. 11)? How was he "blessed"?

Impatience in times of trial is also manifested in swearing. Here it is not a question of profanity, or cursing, primarily. Neither is it a matter of taking an oath in a court of law. The practice forbidden is the thoughtless use of the Lord's Name or some other name to attest the truthfulness of one's speech.... Those who know him should be able to depend on the fact that his yes means yes and his no means no.

17a. In the context of enduring trials, what is (a) the principle and (b) the warning in verse 12?

17b. In what way was Job a good example of controlling his tongue and not allowing extreme circumstances to tempt him to sin in that way? See Job 1:21-22.

Putting My Faith to the Test

- Are you laying up treasures on earth?

- Are your business methods strictly honest?

- Do you live luxuriously, or do you live sacrificially so that others may come to know the Savior?

- Are you getting bitter about the chronic length of your trials … getting bitter with the Lord?

- Are you strengthening your heart by reassuring yourself that you are growing spiritually through your trials? (Are you growing? Reread chapter 1).

- Are you allowing the promise of the Lord's return to comfort your heart?

STUDY ELEVEN

James 5:13–20

Praying, Confessing, and Caring

Faith on Trial

In every circumstance of life, we should go to the Lord in prayer.... We should see God as the first great Cause of all that come to us in life. We should not look into what Rutherford called the "confused rolling of the wheels of second causes." It is defeat to allow ourselves to be victims of circumstances, or to wait for our circumstances to change. We should see no hand but His.

1. How many times does some form of the word "prayer" occur in the remainder of the chapter?

2a. What types of prayer are mentioned between verses 13 and 18? Note the verse numbers.

2b. What is verse 13 basically saying?

3. In a general sense, what is all sickness the result of?

4. What are some means God uses to heal us? Which ones are referenced here in verses 14 and 15?

Praying, Confessing, and Caring

James is not talking about every kind of illness, but only about a certain form of sickness, that is, a sickness which is the result of certain specific circumstances. The key to understanding the passage is found in the words, "and if he has committed sins, he will be forgiven."... It is a definite promise of the Lord that where sickness is a direct result of sin, and where that sin is confessed and forsaken in the manner described, the Lord will heal.

---

5. What are the three promises in verse 15 related to sickness that result from sin?

6. When is it appropriate to confess our sins to one another? What attitudes does that require of me, (a) if I am the offender and (b) if I am the one offended?

More often than we are willing to admit, illnesses are caused by sin—such sins as gluttony, worry, anger an unforgiving spirit, intemperance, jealousy, selfishness, and pride. Sin in the life brings sickness and sometimes death (1 Corinthians 11:30). We should confess and forsake sin as soon as we are aware it has come into our lives. All sin should be confessed to God. In additions, sins against other people should be confessed to them as well. It's vital for our spiritual health and good for our physical health.

Faith on Trial

7a. How does James describe Elijah (vv. 17-18)?

7b. Why was Elijah's prayer "effective" in prompting God to answer as He did (vv. 16-18; Deuteronomy 28:12, 23)?

7c. What is the principle from Elijah's prayer life that relates to praying for people who are sick as a result of God's disciplinary action? See 1 John 5:14-15.

8. What general principles do we learn from Elijah about praying and prayer?

9a. What kind of person is verse 19 talking about?

9b. Describe the person who "turns him back." What is James's encouragement for this person?

10. What place does Elijah's example have in this situation?

Praying, Confessing, and Caring

11. Name some things that hinder us from being more active in restoring backsliders.

How immense is the significance of this ministry! First of all, he saves the erring brother from dying prematurely under the chastening hand of God. Secondly, he covers a multitude of sins. They are forgiven and forgotten by God. Also they are forgiven by fellow-believers and veiled from the gaze of the outside public. We need this ministry today. In our zeal to evangelize the lost, perhaps we do not give sufficient attention to those sheep of Christ who have wandered from the fold.

---

12. Is there a "sinning saint" of your acquaintance to whom you should be reaching out to help restore to spiritual health?

Putting My Faith to the Test

- ✍ Do you "pray without ceasing"?

- ✍ Do you know hymns of the faith and Christian songs well enough to sing them as you go about your day?

- ✍ Do you know God's Word well enough to pray according to His will?

- ✍ When you become ill, whom do you contact first—the doctor or the Lord?

- ✍ When you sin against another person, are you willing to go to him and apologize?

- ✍ When you see a brother fall into sin, do you criticize him or try to restore him?

STUDY TWELVE

James 4: 1–10

REVIEWING JAMES TOGETHER

Faith on Trial

And so we come to the end of this practical little epistle. In it we have seen faith on trial. We have seen faith tested by the problems of life, by unholy temptations, by obedience to the Word of God. The man who says he has faith has been challenged to exhibit it by avoiding partiality or snobbishness and to prove it by a life of good works. The reality of faith is seen in a person's speech; the believer learns to yield his tongue to the Lordship of Christ. True faith is accompanied by true wisdom; the life of envy and strife is exchanged for that of practical godliness.

Faith avoids the feuds, struggles, and jealousies that spring from covetousness and worldly ambition. It avoids a harsh, critical spirit. It avoids the self-confidence which leaves God out of life's plans. Faith stands trial by the way it earns and spends its money. In spite of oppression, it manifests fortitude and endurance in view of the Lord's return. Its speech is uniformly honest, needing no oaths to attest it. Faith goes to God in all the changing moods of life. In sickness, it first looks for spiritual causes. By confession to God and to those who have been wronged, it removes these possible causes. Finally, faith goes out in love and compassion to those who have backslidden.

Reviewing James Together

1. Turn to Study 1, question 8. Has the question you wrote there been answered in the course of the study? If not, pose it to the group when you meet.

2a. If you had been one of those pioneer Jewish believers reading James's letter, how do you think you would have reacted and responded initially?

2b. How would you have been challenged?

2c. How would you have been comforted?

2d. Have you been challenged and/or comforted?

3. Have you learned anything in this study of James that you did not know before? If so, what?

4. Name one lesson that has made an impact on you in your current circumstances, and how.

5. As a litmus test for genuine faith in Christ, name an area in your life this study pinpointed that needed correcting, and how you are going about correcting it.

Your faith and mine are on trial each day. What is the Judge's verdict?

---

6. As a group, describe what genuine, mature faith in Christ should look like to our hostile, unbelieving world. Ask God together for the courage to live this kind of testimony in your community.